SO-AYZ-137

Get Your SHIFT Together

The Secret to Working With Multiple Generations in the Workplace

Bonnie D. Monych, CPC, CM

GENESIS
COMMUNICATIONS, INC.

Get Your "Shift" Together
by Bonnie Delesandri Monych
Copyright ©2010 Bonnie Delesandri Monych

ISBN 978-1-58169-349-2
For Worldwide Distribution
Printed in the U.S.A.

Genesis Communications
P.O. Box 191540 • Mobile, AL 36619
800-367-8203

DEDICATION

I would like to thank my two daughters, Stefanie and Mallory, for providing me with hands-on knowledge of Gen-Xers and Millennials even though they had no idea they were lab rats!

I thank my two granddaughters, Aubrey and Brianne, for their contribution to my continued understanding of whatever we call the next generation to join the Boomers, Gen-Xers, and Millennials in the workplace (I think the Veterans will all be retired by then and with any luck, this Boomer too!)

Table of Contents

Introduction

One of the reasons I decided to write this book was not only to share my professional research regarding this topic, but also to provide individuals with the basic knowledge needed to work effectively and peacefully with all generations at work.

Everyone has differences and similarities with one another. Just because someone acts, looks, and thinks differently than we do, does not mean that we will find it more difficult to work with them. This book is meant to uncover some of the misconceptions (labels) that we impose on those who are different based on age. It will provide an insight to some commonsense factors that contribute to some of the different ideas, behaviors, and attitudes that each generation brings with them to the workplace. This book is designed to provide a quick and easy reference that explains these differences, point out the values of these differences, give some simple suggestions (Prescriptions) on how to work most effectively with each generation . . . and have some fun at the same time!

I am admitting that I am classified as a "Baby Boomer" as I was born in 1950; however, due to some forced behavioral changes I might be considered a "Cusper" (someone who has characteristics and behaviors of two generations) or someone "on the cusp." For me, I move regularly between a Boomer and a Gen-Xer, and if you asked my daughters they might even refer to me as a Veteran. I think that has more to do with my tendency to encourage them to always have "mad money" in their wallets, which was advice passed on to me from my mother, who was a Veteran!

Just to let you know, along with my good friend and colleague, Cynthia Crocker, I conducted numerous focus groups for this project. We had focus groups with only Veterans, only Boomers, only Gen-Xers, and only Millennials. We also had focus groups with all generations mixed together. We asked them numerous discussion questions, tested their generational knowledge, and enjoyed an atmosphere of high energy and great participation. This was a subject about which most participants were passionate.

We even witnessed a "cat fight" between a Boomer female and a Gen-Xer female. The Boomer felt she had earned her way to success by fighting and clawing her way up while hitting the "glass ceiling" frequently but charging on and paving the way for younger women. The Gen-Xer had no apologies for her expectations of success quickly, did not intend to pay her dues, and had no idea why she was supposed to appreciate this Boomer. And so it goes!

In addition, we conducted an electronic generational survey on a global basis for one year. When we began our research, we found very little published information that was more recent than 2001/2002. Since that time, more information has become available on this topic as the impact has forced corporate America to take notice.

The workplace is not only the world of change; we are in need of changing leadership that awakens to the critical skill of embracing and celebrating the strengths of each generation. I hope to provide the reader with a straightforward and "get to the point" reference that will put them on the fast track to understanding and developing this critical skill of generational awareness.

Each and every one of us has our own filters that we look through based upon our gender, culture, religion, race, and age. My experience in working with thousands of people in the workplace has shown me that the one that everyone feels most comfortable talking about is the age filter. This is good news! Discussing our differences and being able to laugh about them is a great start in figuring out how to turn these differences into valuable resources for each of us. Sharing our experiences with one another begins to bridge the gap—the generation gap! This book is intended to begin that process for you and for me. Enjoy it and share it with others!

You will find Doctor Bonnie's Prescription at the end of each section, which will be your bottom-line takeaway as well as a general summary of the key components presented in the chapter. Please know that I am not a medical doctor or Ph.D. My expertise of over twenty-five years working with both employees and employers regarding people issues in the workplace and providing thousands of individuals with Career Strategies that have been successful has rewarded me with being known as Your WorkPlace Doctor on national television and radio and as a speaker.

The following chapters should provide you with the checkup that you need to make your own diagnosis. Enjoy!

CHAPTER ONE

Who Are These People?

What is a generation? Some synonyms for the word are *age group, cohort, age bracket, making, creation, and invention*. I found the combination of these words very interesting. I really like the action ones because you will find that each generation (yes, even the "oldies") bring not only their specific age group, but also valuable action to the workplace. Another interesting thing about generational differences is that even though age falls under the umbrella of diversity, people are more than willing to have engaging conversations about these differences. Other elements of diversity such as culture, religious beliefs, gender, and race are still difficult for most in the workplace to honestly discuss.

A great example of this happened in one of our focus groups. We were discussing some of the labels that we use when referring to the different generations. Two African-American females became extremely heated when talking about the misconceptions of the younger female Gen-Xer with regards to the older Boomer female when it came to career expectations in the workplace. Both women realized that even though they would generally be extremely loyal to the fact that they were both African-American females and would support each other based on this element alone, when it came to generational issues, that loyalty was not the driving factor for them. Once this was pointed out to the group and the two females admitted that this was indeed true, the focus group was open and comfortable debating the good, the bad, and the ugly of generational issues but still cautious when discussing issues of race.

The good news is that we can have wonderfully interesting and frank discussion in this and the following chapters, so relax and prepare to be informed enough to be certain that you will have the information you will need to navigate the choppy waters of working with these four generations effectively and happily. What defines these four generations? Most research utilizes simple birth years.

In 2010:

Veterans   born 1900-1945   *65+ years old*

Boomers   born 1946-1964   *46-64 years old*

Gen-Xers   born 1965-1980   *30-45 years old*

Millennials born 1981-1999   *18-29 years old*

Now within each generation there are *Cuspers*, which means that a person has some of the characteristics of two generations especially if they were born "on the cusp" of one or the other. For example, my oldest daughter was born in 1980, which officially makes her a Gen-Xer; however, because she is only one year away from being a Millennial, she would be considered a Cusper. She has characteristics of both a Gen-Xer and a Millennial.

You should also know that depending on what research you review, multiple names are used for each generation except for the Boomer generation. They are as follows:

- Veterans are also known as Traditionalists, Matures, and Silents.

- Gen-Xers are also known as Generation X, Baby Busters, Latchkey Generation, and Post Boomers.

- Millennials are also known as Generation Y, Generation WHY, Echo Generation, and Net Generation.

For the purpose of this book, we will refer to them as **Veterans, Boomers, Gen-Xers, and Millennials**. You should also know that depending on what research you review, there have been some differences regarding the years used to define each generation. Keeping in mind the Cusper who has characteristics of two generations, we basically have everyone covered.

Of course we know that every single person has unique characteristics, and just because you were born at a certain time does not necessarily make you a Veteran, Boomer, Gen-Xer or Millennial, but certain common stereotypes do exist. Let's look at each generation.

You Can't Teach an Old Dog New Tricks

Veterans: born 1900-1945

In the workplace sometimes we hear these employees called names like "old dogs," "old birds," or "geezers." None of these is very complimentary, but they do describe those employees who seem to be the oldest at work. Remember, with age comes wisdom, so don't be so quick to discount their contribution to the daily grind. Veterans experienced the Great Depression and honored war heroes. For two decades they had the workplace to themselves. They were rewarded for loyalty, hard work, and doing what they were told. Symbols were important to them; God and country provoked emotion. These workers respected authority and the "chain of command" was commonplace at work. Respect was as important as air to breathe. The workplace was industrialized and most men worked eight-to-five.

Home life was considered traditional with wives taking care of home and family. Dad arrived home to a hot meal prepared by Mom, and the children were expected to eat quietly (whatever was put on their plates) and speak when spoken to. Most families watched little or no television as television was a luxury. All children had chores necessary to build responsibility and work ethic. Most families owned one car, which they kept until it would no longer run. Christmas consisted of one or two gifts per child and if lucky, also new underwear, socks, and pajamas. Saving money was critical, and many people kept their savings under the mattress.

My (Veteran) dad was always worried about whether or not his money was completely safe in the bank. Now I must tell you that my very first career was as a banker, and even then he was careful about depositing *all* of his money in the bank. I often assured him that as long as he did not have over $250,000 in any one bank, the FDIC insured that his money was safe. That assurance was not good enough for my dad. He had a safe in his home and hid cash all over his house. Unfortunately, as he grew older he would forget where he had hidden it!

One of the saddest days of my life happened in 2004 when I lost my father in an accident. He left this world exactly as he wanted—working—and when my siblings and I began the arduous task of preparing his home to sell, it was like a monetary Easter egg hunt as we found thousands of dollars stashed all over the house. The mattress obviously was not enough for him! God bless him.

People of this generation knew that for their children to have better than they did, education would be absolutely necessary. For the first time, families spent hard-earned savings on college for their children. Young men were expected to go to college and not war. Young women began to think about college for the first time. This opened the possibilities for women outside of nursing and secretarial school.

Although the world has changed significantly, it is important that you understand this generation's perspective. They have witnessed enormous changes in work ethic, expectations, authoritative direction, technology, and most importantly the influx of generation after generation into the workplace. Remember that for two decades they were the only generation in the workplace. The workplace has gotten very crowded, and they feel their place is not what it once was.

Summary

The **Veteran** (1900-1945) generation is one of great character. They are loyal to a fault. They are dependable and trusted coworkers. Listen to what they have to say; most definitely you will learn something. Don't forget that they need respect, and you should tap into their wisdom. Since people of this generation were mentors long before mentoring programs existed, you would do yourself a favor by asking one to be your mentor. You can trust Veterans to keep confidences, share company history with you, and guide you without expecting anything in return but your listening ear.

Your Prescription Is ...

Ask one or two Veterans to have a cup of coffee with you. Acknowledge their wisdom and experience. Ask them for their advice in dealing more effectively with others in your workplace ... then SHUT UP AND LISTEN.

—*Doctor B*

FLOWER POWER/ MEGA CONSUMERS

Boomers: born 1946-1964

This generation was thrust into the workplace of competition. They are the largest employee population in the world of work. They also created the term *mega consumer* as they gobbled up the notion of bigger is better. They gave the phrase "keeping up with the Joneses" new meaning.

Two income households began to increase substantially as Boomer women joined the rat race shortly after "burning their bras" during the women's movement. More and more women earned undergraduate and graduate degrees. Women were told they could "bring home the bacon and fry it up in the pan," so parents began putting children in daycare; the term *latchkey kid* first appeared on the scene.

As parents, they wanted the best for their children, so guilt took over and children were given only the best that money could buy. Parents continued to work diligently, staying late, coming in early, and always working to make themselves look better than their colleagues. They wanted to ensure their job security in hopes of retiring with a fat financial plan and a gold watch. Then the rug got pulled out from under them!

Mid-career, massive layoffs began in the workplace. They not only lost their jobs but many lost their way. This generation had to retool quickly and jump into the highly competitive job market surrounded by not only their boomer colleagues but also the next younger generation beginning to enter the job market. Loyalty became an old memory, and being technologically savvy was a requirement. This generation had to struggle to keep their heads above financial waters even after years of work experience. The smart ones adjusted and embraced technology, and many others learned a new term, *reinventing yourself*, or embarked upon their second career. The traditional job security their fathers had enjoyed would be forever changed, the divorce rate almost doubled, and their children had front row seats!

People often say that in times of adversity there is always opportunity. This notion proved very true for me and my career. As I have indicated, I am a Boomer. At the time that the rug was being pulled out from under my generation, I was an Executive Recruiter (Headhunter), and needless to say, employers were no longer hiring and certainly not paying placement fees. I retooled my skill set and expanded into a new specialty called *outplacement*. This is a career consulting and job search service provided by employers to laid off workers so that they can learn how to prepare a resume, network, interview effectively, and much more. My skills as a search consultant matching candidates with specific jobs were a natural foundation for learning the outplacement business. At that time, there was a lot of this business to be had. This actually led me into the Human Capital Management Consulting, which I still do to this day! Who knew?

It is important that you remember that this generation is highly competitive, so they are extremely hard working. Face time is very important to them, so one must balance technology with old fashioned one-on-one communication. I have often heard from my Boomer clients that they just don't get why the younger generation of workers can't simply step down the hall to ask a question; they send an email to the office next door! This makes no sense to a Boomer. If you want to make sure you are heard by a Boomer, take that short walk down the hall or to the next floor!

Summary

Boomers (1946-1964) are very good at solving problems. They are both contemplative and optimistic. You can learn a lot if you listen. They can re-direct quickly (remember they got the job rug pulled out from under them), and they have the business maturity that younger generations need. Don't forget that this generation is very COMPETITIVE and they are motivated by challenge.

Your Prescription Is ...

Make a habit of talking with a Boomer face-to-face, don't over-use email; you must build a relationship.

—Doctor B

THE MISUNDERSTOOD
GENERATION

Gen-Xers: born 1965-1980

Often labeled "slackers," this generation is far from it. Many times their need for independence is confused with a lack of responsibility. One must remember that this generation were latchkey kids and became very resourceful. They were raised on technology, so communicating through technology is as natural to them as breathing.

This group is often accused of hiding behind technology, and there is some truth to this. At very young ages they began to utilize their computers for entertainment, information, and communication. This generation became the first to spend many hours each day interacting with a computer screen. They learned quickly how to access information and create their own virtual worlds. Speed and results were a necessity, and patience to them was not a virtue!

This generation was basically shaped by a 24/7 media. They had access to world events real time. They think and communicate in sound bites. They do lack institutional trust (they watched their parents lose their jobs after many years of loyalty), and they have demanded work/life balance.

In one of our focus groups, a gentleman (a Boomer) expressed his intense dislike for these younger (Gen-Xers) workers who clearly and proudly announced that they had lives outside of work and had no intention of working one minute past 5:00. They expected to leave precisely at the time that they were paid for and arrive no earlier than exactly their starting time. Furthermore, they felt that they had more than enough time to complete their work and still have time for "surfing the net." Our Boomer gentleman had to admit that they did indeed get their work done, but he still did not accept their attitude.

Our Gen-Xers explained that based upon the experiences of their parents, they believed that loyalty to the company guaranteed nothing; however, loyalty to oneself provided the only job security that they understood. They believed in working efficiently, doing their jobs, and enjoying their personal lives too. They were not going to sacrifice their relationships with their friends and family for work. They believed in worker smarter, not harder!

Summary

This **Gen-Xer** (1965-1980) generation understands the value of real productivity and does not need to be tied to a desk to prove it! Their independence allows them to be open-minded when it comes to working effectively. Our competitive workplace demands results, and this generation knows how to focus as well as multi-task. They have raised the bar when it comes to work/life quality and can be considered the best technology teachers you can find. Make use of these unique skills. They don't need face time; they want to work with you efficiently. That means utilizing technology at every opportunity. If you don't know how to use email or send an attachment, ask a Gen-Xer to help you. They may laugh, but they enjoy showing off their technology skills.

Your Prescription Is . . .

Let them know that you appreciate their lead in creating work/life balance and ask them for advice on how to create more balance in your work day.

—Doctor B

PRECIOUS CHILDREN

Millennials: born 1981-1999+

This generation is one of the more controversial groups to date. They are often seen as entitled and easily distracted. This group was on the receiving end of parents who took the extreme opposite approach to parenting than the Boomers did and hovered over their children's every need. They were given a vote in just about everything from family vacations to dinner menus. Their parents assisted them with homework, attended every activity, and made sure they were enrolled in the best preschool program. When they competed in sports, everyone was a winner and received a trophy. Every activity was celebrated with fanfare.

This group is also concerned with workplace safety, as they have witnessed school shootings either firsthand or through media; many have had to go through metal detectors at school. They live in a world of drive-by shootings and more violence than necessary. They can be very good collaborators as they believe in the "good for all" theory. They grew up participating in group activities and generally work well with others as was required for promotion through their young educational training. Diversity is an expectation to them, which has created value in the workplace not known before. Many believe that it will be this generation that actually brings true diversity and inclusion to the workplace.

Needless to say, this generation values and requires cutting-edge technology. They are not afraid to ask questions, and they frequently question authority. They expect recognition for what they do again and again. Just the other day, I was talking with a friend (Boomer) who was telling me that as part of his management responsibilities, he was now required to commend and acknowledge in writing when one of his staff members (Millennials) had arrived for work on time for a month. He was not happy about this and could not believe that his employer was requiring such an action. I explained to him some of the reasons that this generation responds more effectively to positive reinforcement than a good old fashioned kick in the butt and why his employer was trying something new. He just shook his head!

Interestingly enough, for the most part, Boomers and Millennials tend to work more effectively with one another then Gen-Xers and Millennials. I will never forget the time that I was consulting with a new executive (Gen-Xer) about the effectiveness (or lack of) of his team. In describing some of the team members, he shared his frustration with the younger team members (Millennials) and described them as "slackers." Yes, that's right—the pot calling the kettle black! For you younger readers, this very old saying means calling someone else by the very same description that could be said of you. (Remember, Gen–Xers are traditionally known as slackers.) It seems our Gen-Xers have much less patience with Millennials than Veterans or Boomers do! All of us tend to forget that we were once the new kids on the block.

Summary

Millennials (1981-1999) want information—fast! Negotiating is second nature to them so they are continually gathering information. The good news is that they are not afraid of change. Ask them for help when learning new technology or even trying to figure out how to do something more efficiently with technology. You can establish a great mentoring relationship with this generation as they welcome your counseling. They are accustomed to seeking input from others and have relied on their parents' guidance their entire life. Don't expect them to pay their dues as it will never make sense to them! This generation has blended work and social life. They will be emailing friends, updating their facebook, and going on e-bay while at work. Texting will be their primary communication tool so you will have to teach them the art of verbal communication— they will need it!

Your Prescription Is ...

Take a Millennial under your wing and explain to them that having lots of information is not the same as having lots of knowledge. Help them understand that business maturity comes from real working experiences and always tell them why!

—*Doctor B*

Notes

Who Are These People?

Notes

CHAPTER TWO

What Do They Want?

Now that we have identified who the generations are, we will now explore what each one wants. Each generation has its own set of needs. Understanding needs—our own and those of others—is critical to working effectively with colleagues. In today's workplace, we are all faced with challenges, stress, and change. We are faced with globalization and changing technology. It is still true that people are an organization's most valuable asset. For the most part, we need to work effectively with people. People are the ones who create, motivate, lead, produce, design, build, and organize the world of work. The more we understand what people need, the more successful we will be.

For example, in my work with thousands of employees and employers I have experienced overwhelming requests regarding resolving communication problems between individuals.

Nine times out of ten the real issue is the need to be heard. Focusing only on your personal communication style and failing to recognize the different needs of others when communicating will land you in hot water more often than not.

Think about tone, cadence, and choice of words when you speak. Would a Veteran find your tone disrespectful? Would a Millennial be thinking, *You are giving me way too much information?* How about that Gen-Xer who only hears sound bites of information. What about the Boomer who really wants you to communicate face-to-face rather than a very brief email? Should you text a Boomer or Veteran? Probably not. I think you can agree why something as simple as understanding the need to be heard can significantly affect your ability to reduce communication problems. Now let's take a look at some of the unique and critical needs of each generation.

Veterans/Traditionalists Need To Be Heard

This generation wants to be heard. They have a tremendous amount of business maturity and knowledge. They have expertise in understanding the value of a dollar. In today's economic meltdown, they can give us all a lesson in living well within our means. So many people complain that our values have gone, that the workplace offers no loyalty, and that respect for authority is a thing of the past. This generation can lead the way in helping other generations bring back these values. They need to see loyalty return to the workplace and hard work rewarded. They need your questions.

I had the pleasure of speaking to an organization that was comprised of "gray hair management," not that you had to have gray hair to belong, but you definitely had to have been employed in the executive ranks for more than twenty-five years. Naturally, this group contained more Veterans than usual. I received a question from a seventy-four-year-old man something like, "Why do people of the younger generation find little or no value in learning their company's history today? It seems like they just want a quick answer and don't have the time to have a real conversation with you."

To a Veteran, taking the time to set the stage before answering your questions is just as important as the answer itself. Another Veteran stopped me after the presentation and asked, "What would you consider to be the single most important issue facing the workplace today?" Now, does that sound like an "old geezer" on his way out the door? I don't think so. Next time you have an opportunity to have a conversation with a Veteran, start listening!

Boomers Need Respect

This generation passed the Equal Rights Amendment, Title IX of the Civil Rights Amendment banning sexual discrimination in schools. This generation created the technology the Xers and Millennials have embraced and taken to an entirely new level. Many believe they stopped a war and changed American politics. They are the largest and best educated group in the workplace. Don't treat them like dinosaurs. Gen-Xers and Millennials should not judge Boomers for their lack of technological expertise, but should offer educational support and training. Boomers need face time, so take the time to speak to them one-on-one, especially regarding urgent issues.

Being a Boomer, I can speak with a certain level of personal experience when I say that when younger generations roll their eyes, we know we are being dismissed! More often than not, we feel like we are raising our children all over again when managing our team.

Many of you probably won't know who Rodney Dangerfield is, but believe me, we often feel just like Rodney, who was known for the phrase, "I get no respect." When one of our employees is not paying attention and texting their buddy during the staff meeting while pretending to be stretching their arms under the table, we feel discounted and yes, irritated. When another employee clears his or her throat and giggles under his or her breath when we ask this individual how to zip a file and send it as an attachment, we feel disrespected and yes, irritated. When an employee is asked to stay at work until a presentation is finished for an important meeting the next day, and they ask if they will be paid overtime, we feel tired and yes, more irritated. Boomers need your respect; they have had a rough road paving the way for younger generations.

Gen-Xers Need Information and Work/Life Balance

This generation believes in the power of information. Asking questions is second nature to them. Boomers may think that asking questions could be seen as questioning authority. Gen-Xers need clear instructions and deadlines. They need opportunities to make decisions, have input, and continual learning. Xers can't be micromanaged and they need to manage as much of their time as possible. Technology is critical and they need to communicate quickly. They need work/life balance and were the first to in-troduce it to employers.

Dude! I will never forget working with a great group of Gen-Xers about how to manage Boomers and Millennials. You would have thought that they were the first and only gener-ation to "feel the pain." One of them asked, "Why does one of my (Boomer) staff members get so irritated when I ask them questions about their work; is it an age thing or are they just in-secure?" Remember when I said that Gen-Xers like to ask lots of questions, and that Boomers often think that Gen-Xers are showing disre-spect when they question their work? Dude! Once I responded with this answer, the Gen-Xer simply responded, "Dude!" More impor-tantly, we understood one another. Another one of our group began complaining about the poor work ethics of his younger (Millennial) team members and then claimed, "They are just slackers!" I said, "Funny thing, my (Boomer) generation actually gave that very label to your generation!" And so it goes.

Remember, if a Gen-Xer is asking lots of ques-tions, most likely they are simply seeking more information. They are information junkies. You see, they focus a great deal on pure produc-tivity—getting the work done as efficiently as possible. That's because they also value work/life balance. Sitting at a desk not really doing anything just makes no sense to them. As Boomers, we thrived on making sure we were the first one at work and the last one to leave because we had to compete with so many others for advancement. It did not matter that we could probably get our assigned work done in half the time; we had to physically be there to be seen by our boss. Times they have changed, and in great part, thanks to the Gen-Xers. They have demonstrated that one can be productive at any time of the day, from almost any location (home/travel/car/pool), and that each person knows exactly what works best for them. I am not saying that corporate America has totally embraced this new idea of the virtual office, but they are getting there—mainly because they have seen the effect on their profit statement. Dude—this Boomer thanks you!

Millennials Need Cutting Edge Technology and Friends To Work With

This generation relies on technology daily. They communicate, produce, think, play, study, and create through it. Their interpersonal skills are not well developed because of it, so they will avoid face-to-face interaction. Confronting a Millennial won't accomplish much. They live in a virtual world, so they prefer you deal with them through technology. They want to join a diverse workforce. They need community and collaboration opportunities.

This generation is also known as Generation Y (Why) because not only do they ask lots of questions like the Gen-Xers, they really don't understand why. Let me explain with an example. I was asked by one of my clients to come and do a "brown bag" session on appropriate dress for the office. Yes, they had a written dress code but as with most company policies, many are not aware that they exist; and if they do, they forgot long ago what they said. This is because over time, many organizations loosen their policies and then all of a sudden, management looks around and wonders what the heck is happening! Such is true in the case of this client that hired me—a growing organization that utilizes lots of technology in what they do and is a part of a very traditional industry.

Many of the employees are Millennials (hence the real purpose of my session). I had prepared a very sharp, entertaining, techno smooth presentation with lots of sound and humor because I knew I would need to entertain Millennials to get them to hear me. The presentation went well. I knew this because the attendees were not checking their BlackBerry's or texting.

When it came time for Q & A, lots of hands raised. In my line of work, lots of questions are a good thing. One of the Millennial staff asked, "Why would it matter what kind of pants or shirt I have on when I work behind a computer most of the day? Isn't the work I produce what is most important?" Good question! You can't expect this generation to understand the subtleties of business etiquette because no one has ever taught it to them. They have lived in a virtual world, built virtual relationships, have had mostly virtual conversations; and now once thrust into the world of people, they have little or no idea about why it is important to their employer that they dress professionally, sitting behind a computer or not!

Yes, there are hi-tech companies that have no dress code but do have nap rooms, and the company fridge has power drinks and beer in it. The break room contains a pool table, game machines, and headsets for music enjoyment; and of course there is a company gym! For most of corporate America today, those amenities are just not available, so our youngest generation will be in need of this very basic training.

I remember learning from a Veteran boss that one should always smile while on the telephone (you remember those black boxes) because your smile effects your tone and how the person on the other end of the line hears you (yes, I said line!). So you see, these gems have been passed down from generation to generation, and so now this Boomer is telling these Millennials that their overall productivity will actually improve when they look and feel professional! If nothing else—**JUST DO IT!**

Summary

At the end of the day, what everyone needs is to enjoy their work, feel respected and appreciated by their colleagues and employers, and to be paid fairly. As they say, easier said than done and actions speak louder than words when it comes to really making an effort to understand each person's individual needs. Try and remember that Veterans need for you to *listen* to them and give them some of your time; Boomers need for you to understand and *acknowledge* the tough knocks that they took to make a better place for you to work and play; Gen-Xers need for you to give them very clear *information* especially about work expectations and then get out of their way and let them create their own working conditions; and finally our Millennials need for you to provide the most *cutting edge technology* and allow them to blend their social and work life, which means that they will be emailing, texting their friends during work hours and might even be more productive with a buddy sitting right next to them.

Your Prescription Is ...

Ask your manager if he/she could arrange for a brown bag lunch focus group on the topic of communicating with different generations. Ask for an outside facilitator if possible so that concrete and specific ideas can be captured. Encourage everyone to put their cards on the table and help each other learn what the other needs. Have fun!

—Doctor B

Notes

CHAPTER THREE

Why Should I Care?

You should care because you will be working with, for, or have them working for you some-time soon if not already. Veterans make up around 8% and shrinking; Boomers around 40%; Gen-Xers 36%; and Millennials 16% and growing. If we looked at the sheer numbers of the three most dominant generations, we would see around seventy-eight million Boomers; around sixty-six million Gen-Xers; and around eighty-three million Millennials. Due to the economic downturn and the "bleeding" of em-ployees' 401k values, many Boomers will not be able to retire as planned and will remain in the workplace some five to ten years longer.

Characteristics of Veterans

Veterans are:
- Traditional
- Conformers

- Respect Authority
- Disciplined
- Savers

Even though there are less and less Veterans in the workplace, you may very well continue to engage with them as a consumer or when volunteering. Believe me, there are many eighty year olds that can outwork many of us younger models! This generation understands the value of work in the work itself. Many are back at work in their second or third careers not just because they need the money but because they feel more useful working. Working is all that most of them have ever known. They hold treasures of information and history.

George (Veteran) had taken a part time job at the local retail store. One of his hobbies had been gardening, and when he heard about a part time position in the gardening department, he quickly applied and got the job. He had worked for a large oil and gas company for thirty-eight years as an engineer, but he really enjoyed helping customers choose the right flowers and vegetables for their gardens. One day his manager, Jeff (Gen-Xer) seemed distracted and unusually short with him. Normally George would simply let it go since Jeff rarely wanted to chat

36

with him, but on this day, he decided to ask Jeff if he could help in any way. After Jeff's initial surprise, he confided that he had received a text message from another employee that they were quitting and would not be back to work. Jeff could not believe that this young (Millennial) employee could be so disrespectful and inconsiderate. George tactfully suggested to Jeff that what he perceived as disrespectful and inconsiderate might be exactly how he (George) might look at Jeff's style of managing him—making no time for conversation and communicating with him only through email. George told him that he respected the fact that Jeff was his manager, and he felt he must do the very best job he could do for him. Jeff and George became very good colleagues after that day.

Tom (Gen-Xer) was an up-and-coming talent with a very large energy company. He had worked diligently for his organization, traveled when needed, and had spent many hours at home on his computer working on reports. He knew that he was being groomed for his boss' VP job and knew that Hank (Boomer) was looking forward to retiring soon and spending some much needed time on his ranch. Everything was in motion when the market crashed, Hank's nest egg dwindled overnight, and his wife was laid off from her job as a paralegal at the age of fifty-eight. Hank could no longer afford to retire as planned, and Tom's long awaited promotion would be put on hold indefinitely. You might want to look around you and see how many Hanks and Toms you work with—or perhaps you are a Hank or a Tom! Pay attention.

Characteristics of Boomers

Boomers are:

- Competitive
- Anti-establishment
- Flexible
- Work Hard
- Believe They Have Paid Their Dues

Learning about each of these generations will provide you with some logical information about how to work effectively with each. You can't run and you can't hide—not for long anyway. Think about it, Boomers were raised by Vets who wanted them to be prosperous so they were pushed to become successful. They had to embrace competitiveness because there were so many of them (seventy-eight million), and not everyone was going to win. They enjoyed Woodstock and were anti-establishment during the Vietnam War, but they ended up being pretty traditional at work.

Boomers believed in working hard, dressing conservatively, and paying their dues. Face time was generally rewarded with advancement. That's why they expect younger workers to earn their way and pay their dues. They are not going to be able to move over anytime soon. As a matter of fact, expect them to work even harder to keep their positions in the workplace.

John (Boomer) had just celebrated his fifty-fifth birthday. He still felt like he was in his early forties as he worked out five days a week and played basketball with a group of guys once a week. He had learned the benefit of technology early on and was easily comfortable with it. This was the first time in John's career that he reported to someone much younger than he was.

Chad (Gen-Xer) was new to the company. He was confident and liked for everyone on his staff to do his or her work with little direction from him. He communicated regularly through email and rarely had meetings with staff. Leaving the office for a couple of hours in the afternoon to attend his daughter's softball games was not unusual.

John began feeling like Chad was avoiding him, was not appreciative of John's working late and coming in early, and did not understand why Chad had not reviewed his work. He was worried that this young guy was phasing him out of the organization. What did John need to do?

John needs to understand that Chad's generation is very independent. They expect that employees will do their jobs; and if they don't, then they will address it with the person but only then. Chad needs to understand that people of John's generation are very competitive and need to know where they stand. Chad needs to know that John finds it awkward to work for someone younger than he and has never even thought about leaving work at 5:00 p.m. or earlier. Their working relationship would be more effective if Chad would take some time to have a few brief face-to-face conversations with John instead of always communicating by email. These simple actions yield huge results!

Characteristics of Gen-Xers

Gen-Xers are:

- Suspicious
- Independent,
- Techno-Heads
- Entrepreneurial
- Self-reliant
- Demand Work/Life Balance

Gen-Xers grew up as latchkey kids. They experienced Watergate, massive layoffs, recession, and the highest divorce rate ever recorded. They also learned to take care of themselves and work independently. Technology was a large part of their upbringing so they learned to be resourceful. They were the first to start demanding work/life balance because they did not want their children to experience what they did. They wanted to be an active part of their children's day-to-day lives. This is why they are very independent at work and can be very creative and entrepreneurial. They know that job security is held within them, so they are always looking to improve their skills. They are comfortable with technology but see it as a tool, not particularly a way of life.

Deborah (Gen-Xer) was having a difficult time working with her current manager. Linda (Boomer) was very controlling and was always looking over her shoulder. She also seemed nervous when Deborah was not in her office and did not understand why Deborah was often out the door promptly at 5:00 p.m. When Deborah asked Linda if she was dissatisfied with her work in any way, Linda said no, she was very pleased that Deborah always met her deadlines and produced exceptional quality.

Deborah used this as an opportunity to let Linda know that she understood their generational differences, asked Linda to allow her some freedom to do her job well, and told her that she would keep Linda informed regularly of her work status. If she were needed to stay after 5:00 p.m. to complete anything that Linda needed, she would be happy to do so. Deborah explained what she needed from Linda to do her best work, and once they understood what was expected of each other, their working relationship turned into an effective collaborative effort.

Don't shy away from sharing your needs and concerns, and always remember to understand the needs of others as everyone can make some adjustments once they realize the benefits. This Boomer was on "automatic" with her managing style, and once the Gen-Xer explained what she needed and how it would contribute to the benefit of both, our Boomer could give this Gen-Xer the independence that she needed.

Characteristics of Millennials

Millennials Are:
- Techno-addicts
- Self-indulgent
- Curious
- Great at multi-tasking
- 24/7 mentality
- Collaborative

- Expect continual learning
- Demand flexibility
- Social
- Must have fun at work

And finally, for our precious Millennials who have grown up on their cell phones, BlackBerry's, laptops, and iPods, their world is global and has few boundaries. Technology is their way of life. Their parents praised them for each and every little accomplishment and included them in most family decisions. They come to the workplace expecting the same. Many say they enter the workplace with a great sense of importance—much more than positive self-esteem. They are used to a collaborative environment, so working on teams is comfortable for them. They are demanding and expect to have fun at work and a chance to do something important right away.

They don't understand paying their dues and will easily tell you that. They will change jobs quickly if it is not to their liking or if they are not provided with the latest in technology. They are multi-taskers and expect to be able to check their Facebook accounts and Twitter during work hours. The Internet plays a pivotal role in their lives. Ask them to do without a TV but never their laptops.

Jet (Millennial) had been working at his very first job as a research analyst for an insurance company for two months. He commended himself on having the skills to find just about any piece of information within minutes, sometimes seconds. He noticed that some of his colleagues (Gen-Xers, Boomers) were not particularly impressed with his technology prowess. He informed his boss (Gen-Xer) that he was much faster, smarter, and more skilled than his colleagues and expected to be promoted with a pay increase within the next few months. His boss shared with him that his colleagues were much more experienced, had more tenure, and suggested that he could learn a few things from them if he would try having a conversation with them once in a while.

Jet sat in the cubicle next to Sam (Boomer) and had tried to text him several times but never received a response. He had copied Mary (Gen-Xer) on a few email blasts, but she never responded either. As far as he was concerned, he had tried to have a conversation with them! What is Jet not getting? He has not taken the time to understand the different needs (especially when it comes to communicating) of different generations.

Jet also genuinely doesn't understand why he is not due for a promotion and pay raise. Our

Boomer manager could have spent some time helping Jet understand the big picture and why he would need to establish some patience and business maturity. Jet is ripe for mentoring and would welcome the guidance. Perhaps Jet could identify a Veteran that could give him some coaching and share his wisdom and experiences, which would help Jet fast track the business maturity that he will need.

Most of us don't always notice the wealth of resources (people) that surround us at work. Too often we live in our own very small world. We tend to associate with others like us. We go to lunch with our friends who are like us. We sit next to our colleagues like us at meetings. Just imagine how much we could learn if we took the time to have lunch with old Harry who sits down the hall from you. What he knows is not written down anywhere, and he knows a lot!

Let's Eat Soup

Put all of these people that I have described together, and you have a big mixed up pot of fabulous soup, which if overheated, will most definitely boil over and create a big mess! On the other hand, it can also be the most original and best tasting dish ever if cooked properly, at the right temperature, and with the appreciation and inclusion of *all* of the ingredients.

Summary

Some of the best dishes are a combination of the most unlikely ingredients. Why not be adventurous and try something different? You might surprise yourself and realize that you have a new appreciation for this new dish called Generational Soup. Why don't you be the chef at your workplace and start a discussion about these generational ingredients and get the dish going.

Your Prescription Is ...

Making sure that you are being heard and understood is important to each of us no matter what generation we represent. Take a proactive role in sharing what you need from others and asking what they need from you, and you will be very surprised how the combination of those differences now work in your favor.

—Doctor B

Notes

CHAPTER FOUR

How Do We Manage Them?

As the Veterans rapidly leave the workplace and the Millennials rapidly arrive in the workplace, it is very likely that Boomers, Gen-Xers and Millennials will be "mixing it up" at work, even though Boomers likely will be managing Gen-Xers and Millennials. Gen-Xers will also be managing Millennials and Boomers. I thought it important to give you some helpful tips on managing Boomers, Gen-Xers, and Millennials, but also give you some ideas about managing Veterans as well.

You know how you get an instruction manual or users guide with the purchase of appliances, tools, and electronics? Have you ever thought to yourself, *Man, I wish Susie or John came with an instruction manual* when finding it difficult or impossible to manage either one of them? This is as close as I can get to providing you with that guidebook to managing each of these generations. No small print included!

Managing Veterans:
Listen To Me

According to Bruce Talgan, who wrote *Managing the Generation Mix* in 2001, most retirees were Veterans. Those retiring at age seventy were born in 1931; those at age sixty-five, in 1936; those at age sixty-two, in 1939. By 2011, there will virtually be no members of this cohort left in the workplace. Now, Bruce Talgan wrote his book long before our current economic crisis, which means that many Veterans are still in the workplace. Some are in their second or third career lives (Wal-Mart greeters come to mind); but they are still part of our productive workforce, and you will most likely have the opportunity to manage them.

Veterans lived in a workplace of rules, procedures, process, and above all hierarchy. Chain of command was the only way to work. Many are still wondering what happened to loyalty, commitment, and respect for seniority. The good news is that if you have the title of Manager, they will understand that you have authority and for the most part, respect that position. They may not respect you. They are still willing to make sacrifices for the company and don't understand why younger generations do not.

Walter has arrived early for the staff meeting, poured his coffee, and is patiently waiting for others to arrive. Slowly the staff files into the room. Around ten minutes after the meeting is scheduled to begin, someone comes in and announces to the staff that their twenty-two-year-old Operations Supervisor has called to say, "Start the meeting without me; I overslept. I'll be there as soon as I can." Walter just doesn't understand—and he never will—how this behavior could possibly be acceptable from a superior.

WHAT YOU NEED TO KNOW:

1. Take the time to listen to them.
2. Give them clearly defined expectations.
3. Show them respect for their contributions.
4. Allow them time to grasp new technology and provide written directions.
5. Give them the opportunity to have input in decision making.
6. Ask them for advice.
7. Make sure that you provide them with standardized policies, procedures, and templates in mind.
8. They believe, "If it's not broken, don't fix it."
9. They don't require any deep meaning from their work.

10. They believe in an honest day's work for an honest day's pay.

Managing Boomers:
R-E-S-P-E-C-T

According to Tom Brokaw author of *Boom*, they were the largest, the best educated, and the wealthiest generation in American history. More importantly, many believe they had liberated the country from the inhibited and inhibiting sensibilities of their parents.

Being a Boomer myself, I can sympathize with my cohorts when faced with being managed by the younger generation. One day I was working with a Boomer on some strategies for improving his team's performance when his Gen-Xer manager interrupted with an urgent request. He asked if she could wait until we were done with our meeting as we were almost ready to wrap it up, but she said no.

He excused himself and asked me to wait. When he returned he was very flustered by her urgent need to speak to him as it seems that she was leaving for the afternoon to have some "me time" and just wanted to know if he could finish the reports needed for tomorrow's board meeting without her input. Naturally, we had a laugh and continued with our work. It seems patience is indeed a virtue! This Boomer just can't respect a manager who seems to take her work so casually. He felt disrespected by her "urgent" interruption and won't be likely to fulfill her request the next time.

WHAT YOU NEED TO KNOW:

1. They have paid their dues throughout their career and want their current contributions to be recognized.

2. Don't treat them like dinosaurs.

3. Show them respect even if they are your subordinates.

4. Ask them for their advice based on their extensive experience.

5. Give them technology and educational support so they are not afraid of it, and don't judge them for their lack of technological expertise.

6. Because they are competitive, they love work challenges.

7. Find a way for them to stand out in the crowd as they have been obsessed with this due to their large peer group.

8. They like to make a difference and this should be considered a prime motivator.

9. Face time is important to them so make sure that you give them personal attention.

10. Flexibility has become important to this generation.

Managing Gen-Xers
I-N-D-E-P-E-N-D-E-N-C-E

This generation grew up in an era of feminism, divorce, and stay-at-home moms being the exception and not the rule. They have created a workplace that is just now beginning to understand their commitment to the term *family-centric* rather than work-centric as was most prevalent in the past. They single-handedly have changed the horizon of work/life balance.

This generation is likely the most highly educated generation ever, but also the first generation in America likely to have a standard of living below that of its parents. Since they were the first generation to earn a report card grade for "works well with others," they tend to be excellent team members and are willing to collaborate. According to *Managing the Generational Mix* by Carolyn A. Martin Ph.D. and Bruce Tulgan, a Gen-Xer explained it this way, "We are the products of high divorce rates, the eighties Reaganomics era, and post-war parents. Every day we are making efforts [to create] well-being and a safe future by working on environmental issues, social acceptance, and lower crime rates." For the most part, attitudes of the Xers and Boomers are galaxies apart.

This generation is accomplishment driven in all facets of their lives. They expect to be successful, and they are committed to making sure that their children never experience the "abandonment" that they experienced. Don't get in their way; they know how to be productive!

I have managed many Gen-Xers in my time, and I can tell you that it will be much easier if you pay close attention to their need for independence. I once had a staff member, let's call her Sally, that I thought was extremely arrogant. She seemed insulted when I questioned her about anything. I quickly realized that once I had let her know what I wanted and when, I simply needed to get out of her way and let her do her job. She needed little supervision and was much more productive when left alone. I later realized that what I had confused with arrogance was independence. She came to me when she had a question or needed more information. She ended up being one of my best employees ever!

Remember, Gen-Xers need lots of room to manage themselves (they have been doing it since childhood) and working traditional eight-to-five is not always what will work best for them. Seek their input with regards to their most productive schedule, and try to make it work.

WHAT YOU NEED TO KNOW:

1. Abandon the "slacker" myth.

2. Distinguish between arrogance and independence.

3. Build corporate cultures that value the individual.

4. Set clear deadlines for tangible end products.

5. Provide them with as much information as you can.

6. Treat their questions as opportunities to teach.

7. Outline and clearly define goals.

8. Let them manage as much of their time as possible.

9. Build constant feedback loops.

10. Make feedback frequent, accurate, specific, and timely.

Managing Millennials
W-H-Y

This generation was raised, by and large, by active, involved parents. They had very protective Boomer and Xer parents who wanted to make sure their children would grow up safe and be treated well. The term *helicopter parent* was awarded to their parents. This generation was infused with self-confidence, and many believe they can leap tall buildings! They are accustomed to having their opinions not only listened to but valued. Hierarchy is not a part of their world; therefore, they are comfortable asking questions of authority figures and expecting an answer.

This generation is connected 24/7, and they have learned to be interdependent. They have spent much time volunteering in their communities, and in one Roper Survey when Millennials were asked for the major cause of problems in the U.S., they answered *selfishness*. This generation is inclusive and used to being organized as teams—and making certain that no one is left behind. They expect their workplace to be fair to all. They will be the first generation to make *true diversity* a reality. They want to know how they, as well as their work, fit into the big picture.

This generation will change jobs if they are not challenged, if they are not having fun, and if they are not allowed the flexibility that they need. They are not afraid to try new things or transition into an entirely different career. Learn from their ease with technology and listen to their ideas; they have something valuable to contribute.

Meet Elaina, a bright eighteen year old that has just started her first job in retail. She hopes to be promoted to Store Manager soon as she thinks she has some great ideas about how to create a more comfortable environment for the store. After working for a couple of months, she believes that the standard corporate guidelines for operations are way too confining. She believes that customers want to feel as though the salesperson is their best friend and suggests that customers be encouraged to just kick back, enjoy the music, and maybe have a cappuccino. Even though this is an upscale clothing store, she feels that they need some couches and comfy chairs, some fashion magazines, and much more funky clothes.

Elaina feels that her manager is stuck in the past and has not been responsive to her suggestions, so she sends the Regional Vice President an email outlining her ideas and suggesting he get back to her quickly. Sound familiar? Unfortunately for Elaina, her first job did not last long, but her manager learned an important lesson about this youngest generation. They need direction and guidance as they mistake information for knowledge, and your job as a manager is to make sure they are given the business knowledge to go with all of that handy information.

WHAT YOU NEED TO KNOW:

1. They want and need clear leadership and role models at work.

2. Mentoring relationships should be two-way to be effective.

3. They want to be challenged. They are looking for growth, development, and continual learning more than they desire money.

4. They want to enjoy and have fun with their coworkers. Acknowledging the social aspects of work, their friends are a priority.

5. Even though they haven't been around a long time, treat their ideas respectfully.

6. Be flexible! This generation "works to live," so they are not going to give up activities because of the job. A rigid schedule will force them to exit.

7. Don't expect them to pay their dues by putting in time. They focus on productivity. Reward them for it.

8. Design office spaces so Millennials are set up physically to share ideas.

9. Encourage them to improve on their communication skills and clearly define the benefit for them to do so.

10. Provide state of the art technology and know that they will be checking their Facebook and Twittering while at work.

The interesting thing is that the Millennials and Boomers seem to understand each other much better. In "Mastering People Management," *Financial Times*, November 19, 2001, Karen Cates and Kimia Rahimi, shared this statement: "A sixty-something graduate recently reflected: 'We wanted what they want. We just felt we couldn't ask.' Herein lies the truth: what young workers want isn't so different from what everyone else wants. However, young workers are asking for it."

The real "rub" has come between the Xers and the Millennials. Gen-Xers complain that the Millennials are another indulged generation like the Boomers. Who would have thought?

Summary

Appreciate new math! One plus one plus one equals 100. That's right, together we can all work more effectively and more importantly, be much happier. Learn the basic needs of each generation: Veterans need for you to listen to them; Boomers need your respect; Gen-Xers need independence; and Millennials need to know why.

Your Prescription Is ...

I know that many believe work is not supposed to be enjoyable. My old and wise Italian dad once said to me when I wanted to change careers because I wasn't enjoying my work, "Work is not supposed to be fun; that's why they call it work. Get a hobby!" He was a Veteran! Make copies of "what you should know" for each generation in this chapter and put them somewhere you can see them each day. After all, that's how "Shift" Happens!

—Doctor B

Notes

How Do We Manage Them?

Notes

CHAPTER FIVE

Communicating With Generations

The art of communication includes many elements. While most of us think immediately of verbal communication, surprisingly, only 40 percent of communication is actually verbal. Included in the other 60 percent is nonverbal such as gestures, expressions, posture, tone, pitch, tempo, rhythm, and even breathing. The most important form of communication is listening. Wilson Mizner once said, "A good listener is not only popular everywhere, but after a while he gets to know something."

In my numerous years of practice, when clients call to engage our firm to help them with a people issue, they usually share with us what kind of problem they are having. They might say that a particular team is not performing effectively or that two employees are not able to work with one another, or perhaps they have a manager who is frustrated with a poorly performing department. Sometimes, they have had employees file formal complaints against their supervisors. Whatever the motivation for the call, we label it our client's POP, an acronym for point of pain. Once we conduct our due diligence, I would tell you that nine out of ten times the originating issue can be traced back to a communication problem! That is why this very element is so important. The following will provide you with some specific tips on each generation's communication style and needs.

Veterans Communication Style:
"Let me tell you a story . . ."

Veterans are traditionalists. They believe in God and country. They give and expect respect, and that includes respectful communications. Rolling your eyes, checking your cell phone or BlackBerry while communicating with this generation will get you nowhere fast!

The most important aspect to communicating with Veterans is to listen patiently to what they have to say. They will not utilize email as a routine method of exchanging information; picking up the phone will serve you better with this generation. Whenever possible, face-to-face conversations are preferable. Don't forget that many of this generation do not utilize email at all, so texting is most definitely not an option!

Joe (Veteran) was a longtime employee of a privately owned manufacturing company. He had worked for three generations of the family including the current CEO (Gen-Xer). Joe was in charge of distribution and knew just about every vendor by first name. Joe worked for this company during a time when a handshake was as good as a signed contract.

One day he received an email from a young (Millennial) sales rep, which seemed to be a string of words, all caps, and made no sense to Joe. He picked up the phone and called the young sales rep and asked him to return his call so that they could talk about what the sales rep needed in his email. That afternoon Joe received another email; this time he sensed that the sales rep was frustrated because this email contained less information and again all caps. He decided that a face-to-face conversation would be more helpful than a phone call, so he walked down to the first floor and located the salesperson standing in the break room punching keys on his BlackBerry.

Joe approached the sales rep and asked him about the two emails. Without looking up, the sales rep simply said, "Don't you know how to read your email? I was trying to save some time, but now that you are here. . ." Now why might you think that these two people might not have a good working relationship? This young sales rep (Millennial) showed no respect for authority, gave Joe little if any time or information, but expected him to respond only one way—his way! Veterans have valuable information to share; they need for you to listen to them and give them your respectful attention.

Boomers Communication Style:
"Let's get to know one another."

Boomers are relationship oriented. Trust is important to them, and they like to get to know you before they are comfortable with real communication. They are generally sympathetic listeners. Since they are competitive and achievement oriented, they like to be heard. This generation was forced to embrace email as one of the elements of workplace communication; however, they prefer face-to-face.

Boomers are more likely to pick up the phone and call you than simply sending you an email. If you work on the same floor with a Boomer, take a walk and personally speak with that individual. It will go a long way toward building that relationship with that person, and he or she will be much more likely to hear what you have to say. When emailing this generation, pay attention to your grammar, tone, and form. Utilize the person's first name and close with yours. This small effort shows you value them enough to take the time for some formality. You will need to check with Boomers before texting them, as this form of communication is not widely utilized by this generation.

David (Boomer) really liked working with the younger generations as he felt he had a lot of experience to share. He had the proverbial rug pulled out from under him after twenty-one years of employment with a large oil and gas company. After he was laid off, he was faced with having to find a job for the first time since college. He learned quickly that the job market had changed, and he was competing with younger and younger candidates.

After successfully landing a new job, he would do everything he could to keep it. One of the biggest challenges that David faced was trying to get to know his colleagues, as it seemed that they were always buried in their laptops or BlackBerry's. Sitting down for a face-to-face conversation was almost never done. He found that even in meetings, individuals were still utilizing their BlackBerry's for communicating even with the guy sitting next to them! David knew that in order to build relationships with his colleagues, he was going to have to embrace technology and look for opportunities to have old fashioned conversation. David had recognized that he needed to be sensitive to the communication needs of his younger colleagues. David is one smart cookie! You can be too.

Gen-Xers Communication Style:
"Sound bites please."

Gen-Xers are multi-taskers and very results oriented, and their communication style reflects exactly that. They are generally brief and direct, and prefer that others communicate with them efficiently. They focus on getting things done, so taking time to establish a relationship with them is not necessary. They use technology as a tool, so they like to communicate via technology. They prefer email, instant messaging, or texting rather than phone or face-to-face communications. They like to get information summarized with as little detail as possible. If they want more information, they will ask for it.

Paying close attention to the formality of your email is unnecessary; Gen-Xers are looking for sound bites and getting to the critical information quickly. Spending time building relationships is reserved for a select few colleagues, so don't think that you have to be their friend to work and communicate effectively with them.

I worked with a Gen-Xer manager who was very efficient. He walked fast, talked fast, even ate fast! One day he shared with me his struggle with one of his staff members (Boomer) that always seemed not to clearly understand what the manager was asking him to do. In talking more with our Gen-Xer, he admitted that his primary method of communication was via email and texting, and that the rest of his staff did not have a problem understanding his direction. He rarely had staff meetings as he felt they were entirely too time consuming. He knew that this (Boomer) staff member was well qualified and that his work was usually exceptional, but he was not comfortable with his lack of understanding of direction.

Once I spoke with the (Boomer) staff person, it became clear that this person needed a little more face-to-face contact with the manager. I suggested that the manager take five minutes a few times a week to stop in this Boomer's office and just check in with him. Although this seemed like a tremendous task for the Gen-Xer manager, he agreed to give it a try. He called me a couple of weeks later to tell me that this had worked miracles. Yes, it was a pain, but it was definitely worth the time! If you want performance from your staff, you must consider their needs!

Millennials Communication Style:
"Instant and Virtual."

Millennials are easily distracted and have grown up in a virtual world. They know very little about building traditional relationships and that includes their communication style. They expect to have lots of input and enjoy input from others. They love information from all directions and can handle multiple forms at the same time. When you are communicating with a Millennial via email, they are probably texting and/or instant messaging at the same time and checking out the latest YouTube video. This doesn't mean that they are not listening to you; they actually have developed this ability. They are very casual communicators. Formality is lacking in any of their communication forms. Collaboration is important to them, so they will solicit many ideas and opinions of others. They prefer to work and communicate with people they like. They build relationships virtually with people all around the world. They prefer as little face-to-face communication as possible.

They text much more than they talk on their

phones. Because they have been raised on technology, they have not developed traditional, business appropriate communication skills. Don't be surprised if they ask their Boomer manager to be their friend on Facebook.

This is one of my most recent and favorite stories that a very good client shared with me. She had hired a very young and sharp Millennial for her insurance company. My client knew that this person's technology skills would be invaluable to the entire team. Montgomery had been working for about two months when she approached my client about a promotion. She explained that she felt that her colleagues were slow and methodical, and that she could "work circles around them." The client asked Montgomery what she had learned about the insurance business and more importantly what she knew about their customers. Montgomery responded, "What does that have to do with my specific job?" As my client chuckled to herself, she told her new hire that perhaps it might be a good idea to pair her up with one of the older and more knowledgeable employees who could mentor her in business acumen while Montgomery, in return, could share her technology expertise. She said that after many months perhaps they could revisit her request for a promotion. She explained that performance had many measurements, and the ability to work well with others who might be different was one of them. Montgomery quit the next day and asked my client for a "letter of recommendation"!

Summary

Learning the communication style of each generation will most definitely help; however, really understanding the "whys" will provide you with more clarity and patience. Remember that Veterans need time to tell you the story, Boomers need face-to-face communication to build relationships, Gen-Xers need sound bites because they are focused on results, and Millennials need instant and virtual as they do not possess the interpersonal skills that are needed in the workplace.

What is important is that your goal in communicating to each person is to make sure that they hear your message and that you hear theirs. Once you figure out how to do that, it won't really matter what form of communication you choose to utilize.

Your Prescription Is . . .

If you work with a Veteran (sixty-five years old+), have face-to-face or phone conversations with them; if you work with Boomers (age forty-six to sixty-four years old) build a relationship with them by talking face-to-face or phone preferably and show respect in your email by utilizing etiquette; if you work with Gen-Xers (ages thirty to forty-five) utilize your email with concise and specific sound bites; if you work with Millennials (ages eighteen to twenty-nine) text urgent requests and follow up with an email with more info.

—Doctor B

Notes

Notes

CHAPTER SIX

Where Is the Rub?

Remember that you really should focus on the value of differences even though it often feels like taking a skid on some very hard concrete. Hence the rub! I think it's best to simply explore some of the primary differences when it comes to your workplace. Putting things out on the table is sometimes the most effective approach to opening up that all-important communication factor that we talked about in chapter 5. Let's take a look at some common stereotypes of each generation, and then we can have some fun . . . and dispel some of those myths as well.

Veterans:
Cornerstone of the Workplace

For the most part, Veterans created the workplace as we moved from an Agricultural Age into an Industrial Age. It was a time of war, of saving, and most importantly of God and country. The organizational design was paternal and that of hierarchy, similar to the military. The corporate rules were clear and everyone played the game accordingly. The workplace was comprised primarily of white men, so diversity was not even on the horizon. The divorce rate was almost nonexistent, and very few women worked outside the home. The workplace belonged to them.

Some Common Stereotypes

- You can't teach and old dog new tricks.
- They should be retired.
- Talk, talk, talk.
- "When I was your age, I . . ."
- Dogmatic and stubborn.
- Waste not, want not.
- Old and worn out.

Boomers:
Changing the World

Boomers were the first generation that came to the workplace with advanced education. They were also a part of a massive workforce (i.e. boom in birth rate) and therefore had to be very competitive. In their youth, they challenged government, traditional institutions, and just about everything that their forefathers valued. (Sound familiar?) Once they entered the workplace, they were forced to comply with the traditional/Veteran values and ethics that the Veterans had established; however, they were the first generation to be joined by women. In order to progress through the organizational hierarchy, they competed aggressively and followed the traditional chain of command. Although many would have liked to challenge the status quo, they simply could not afford the risk.

Women began learning about "the glass ceiling." Money was not a problem as this generation became the wealthiest and therefore began to acquire assets far beyond what their parents had envisioned. The term *McMansion* was actually coined for them. They became known as *super consumers*.

Midway through many of this generation's career track, the rug was pulled out from under them and job security became an elusive dream of the past. They went through downsizing, rightsizing, cost reduction, and the new fear of looking for a job (with hundreds of their coworkers). Talk about retooling; this generation had to become experts in acquiring all kinds of new skills. Thus they are frequently misjudged.

Some Common Stereotypes

- Workaholics.
- Guild ridden parenting style.
- Suffer from technology phobia.
- Face-time equals performance.
- Slow to change.
- Values only material things.
- Corner office motivated.

Gen-Xers:
Self-reliant

This generation is one of the most misunderstood of all of the generations. They were raised during a time of the highest divorce rate and consequently became known as latch-key kids because they had to return home from school to an empty house and many times take care of younger siblings. They had to discipline themselves to do their homework, do their chores, and at times start dinner. They had already taken care of themselves for several hours when their parents returned home in the evening.

Technology became a common tool for this generation. They clearly considered it a tool, not a social outlet. They were shaped by a world of 24/7 media and were bombarded with continual messages. This generation introduced work/life

balance to the workplace as they were deter-
mined to show the world that you could have
both a successful career and a family life. For the
first time, employers heard the demands of flexibility from their employees. They weren't going
to miss their children's lives.

Some Common Stereotypes

- Slackers.
- Not work motivated.
- All are tattooed and pierced.
- Hide behind technology.
- Aloof.
- Always pushing the envelope.
- I want it NOW.
- Dude!

Millennials:
Why Not?

The Millennials were the benefactors of the turn
of the millennium when Americans moved the
spotlight back onto kids and their families.
During the post-WWII time, children were all
the rage. It was a great time to have kids and to
be a kid. When Gen- Xers were growing up,
this was not the case. As we have learned, they
did most of their growing up on their own. The

early nineties saw the spotlight swinging back to families. The Federal Forum on Family Statistics reported the national attention to children was at an all-time high.

This is also the most scheduled and structured generation ever. As children, Millennials had parents and teachers micromanage their schedules and lives. Free time became obsolete. In addition, this generation has seen violence from the bombing in Oklahoma to the Columbine tragedy. Many even had to go through metal detectors at their schools.

This generation grew up in a global world connected to technology 24/7. Their parents were so active in their lives that many times they championed causes on behalf of their children. Now we know when surveyed, Millennials actually say they like their parents, which is very different from all previous generations. It could be because they are accustomed to being rewarded and acknowledged just for breathing (well almost). They do believe that they are indeed very special.

When entering the workplace, they have continued to expect those accolades and believe they can and should question and/or challenge authority. After all, they questioned their parents about everything and negotiated with them regularly. They are optimistic that their generation will really change the workplace environment where basketball courts, power nap rooms, and refrigerators filled with your choice of beer, power drinks, and iced lattes will become the norm.

Some Common Stereotypes

- Entitled.
- Easily distracted.
- What's next?
- Live in a virtual world.
- Inexperienced with life.
- Wants it all and wants it NOW, if not, WHY?
- Little or no communication skills.
- Lazy and spoiled.
- ADD (Attention Deficit Disorder) generation.

So, where is the rub? As you can see from the common stereotypes of each generation, each and every one of us has our idiosyncrasies and our unique gifts and talents. It is just human nature to shy away from those who are unlike us and move toward those who are more like us. So that tells us that it is much more about the unknown than the actual difference.

In one of our focus groups that contained individuals from each generation, we experienced an interesting observation. In the beginning of the session, people were told that they could sit anywhere they wanted. Naturally, those who knew each other (only a few) sat together, and most of the others sat next to someone that appeared to be their same age. So we had Veterans sitting together, Boomers, Gen-Xers, and Millennials. It was even apparent that the Veterans and Boomers seemed to be on one side of the room and the Gen-Xers and Millennials on the other side.

As most focus groups are conducted, we began with some open-ended questions. Veterans and Boomers were more likely to raise their hand to speak, Gen-Xers and Millennials shouted out their comments willy-nilly. It was an energized discussion. For our lunch break, we had assigned seating with a good mix of all generations at each small round table. This was not a working lunch, so each table was able to talk about whatever they wanted. We observed lots of conversation at each table.

When the group returned to our discussion room, people then chose to sit next to those with whom they had eaten lunch. Now we had a good mix of each generation around the room. What we discovered was that even though in the earlier session there was clearly an aversion to those generations perceived to be different from themselves, once the group was forced to get to know those who were from a different generation at lunch, the preconceived labels or stereotypes that we heard from each generation had significantly changed. We observed more politeness, more consideration, more listening. This clearly came from getting rid of the unknown by learning more about the individual and understanding the whys behind each of us. Try it; you'll like it!

Summary

Variety is the spice of life! We all have preconceived notions about each of these four generations; some of them may be well-deserved and others a figment of our imagination. Each individual brings a wonderful blend of life experiences to the workplace. Our Veterans are the cornerstone of the workplace and yes, they do like to talk; Boomers truly changed the world and yes, they are workaholics; Gen-Xers are self-reliant and yes, they are always pushing the envelope; and Millennials do ask why not (a lot) and yes, they are easily distracted. But isn't that wonderful? What a fabulous blend of humankind.

Your Prescription Is . . .

If you are smart, and I know that you are, make an effort to try and figure out how to work effectively with each individual. Doing this will make your work life the best place for you.

—Doctor B

Where Is the Rub?

Notes

Notes

CHAPTER SEVEN

Tales From the Workplace

Now that you have learned a little something about each of the four generations, it is time for you to test your knowledge. I am going to tell you some real stories from my experiences in the workplace. The names have been changed to protect the innocent (legal note: liability), and the specific details regarding the organizations may vary; however, each narration actually happened. Pay close attention to each description as you will be asked a few questions at the end of each. Obviously, I won't be able to grade you, so I want you to grade yourself. Remember the purpose of this is to give you some idea about what you have learned so far. Grab a cup of coffee, tea, or whatever suits your pleasure and continue reading.

Once upon a time in a land not far away . . .
There were two Asian-American professionals

working in the customer service department of a large energy provider. The department manager was concerned about their continual interpersonal issues. One of the Asian-American females had been born and raised in her mother country by her grandmother and was very traditional in her work habits. The other female who was close in age had been born and raised in the U.S.A. by her very young mother.

The department manager did not understand why they were not working well together; after all they were of the same culture and close in age. Both were good workers but very different in the way they communicated with one another. He felt that they made it clear that they did not like each other, but the overall productivity of the department depended upon a good working relationship with all colleagues in the department.

Question: Do you think this could be a generational issue? If so, why?

Question: What kind of generational influences might have contributed to these two employees?

Question: Can cultural and generational influences be the same?

Question: What would you do to help these two employees understand their communication differences?

***Hint from Doc B**—All of us are influenced
by our parents, so their age or generation has
an impact on who we are.*

Once upon a time in a land not far away . . .

A very frustrated young school teacher named
Gloria had been teaching for three years at a ju-
nior high not far from where she lived. She really enjoyed the children and the new challenges
that they brought with them each year.
Although a few colleagues were around her age,
most of the teachers were much older than she.
She was a very creative teacher and enjoyed
sharing her many ideas with her teaching team.
It seemed to her that the more experienced
(older) teachers would shoot down each and
every idea that she would suggest. They often
used an old saying; "If it isn't broken, don't fix
it."

Just recently, her school began undertaking a
very large computer system upgrade, and she
was asked to be the lead on the project for her
school because the school principal had observed her efficient computer skills. Excited to
begin the implementation process, she carefully
explained in an email to her fellow teachers
what the process would entail along with what
would be expected of them. She clearly listed
the action items and the dates that each should
be completed.

To her surprise, most of her fellow teachers had not completed their tasks by the deadline. She sent another email reminder and that afternoon in the teacher's lounge, she had an opportunity to ask several teachers about their lack of response to her requests. A couple of older teachers explained that they did not regularly check their school email as it had not been a very good resource for them and that they usually got a note or memo regarding such things. Therefore, they were not even aware of the system implementation project.

Other teachers shared that although they had read the email, they were embarrassed to admit that they did not understand the instructions, and one admitted that she was waiting on her grandson to show her how to complete the tasks. Gloria was shocked and dismayed at what she felt was their determination to not make any changes. She shared her concerns and frustrations with her school principal (also older) and learned that she was not at all surprised by their reactions.

Question: *What could Gloria have done to communicate more effectively?*

Question: *What could the older teachers have done to build a better working relationship with Gloria?*

Question: *What could the principal have done to facilitate the effective communication to all teachers regarding this system conversion?*

Hint from Doc B—*Technology is a generational challenge and so is building trust.*

Once upon a time in a land not far away . . .
Jack was soon turning sixty-three years old and had worked for his transportation company for many years. He had supervised and trained any number of new employees over these many years. He understood that each person had a learning curve and was accustomed to a significantly improved performance after about six months.

Jack had begun to complain that over the past three or four years, the new employees being sent to his department seemed less and less qualified to do the most basic of skills required. He also noticed that the learning curve had begun to exceed the usual six months time frame. He also noted that when he expressed his disappointment, these new hires were insulted by his audacity to speak to them in this way. Many times when Jack was talking to these employees, they were so engrossed in their cell phone screens and busily checking their emails that he had implemented a new rule about when they could use their cell phones during work hours. He believed he had to hold their hands constantly and felt like he was raising children all over again!

Management reassured Jack that they were recruiting only the best and that many of these employees came from the top schools in the country. They were hiring the cream of the crop. Jack felt that if this was the cream of the crop, he was really looking forward to retiring in two years!

Question: *What kind of generational issue, if any, was Jack dealing with?*

Question: *How would you have coached Jack to deal more effectively with his new employees?*

Question: *Do you think Jack communicated effectively to management regarding his concerns? If no, what might he have done differently?*

Question: *Why were the new employees shocked that Jack spoke to them about his disappointment in their work performance?*

Hint from Doc B—*Each generation hears differently; Millennials have lots of knowledge but little experience.*

Once upon a time not far away...

Stacy had recently joined a marketing company that was ranked number one in their industry. She had been recruited from college and had actually worked at the company as an intern for two summers. She was a wiz with media technology and was thrilled to be able to work with their state of the art technology. Several people in Stacy's department had many years of experience and expertise. Her manager was in his mid-thirties and traveled extensively. Once Stacy got the lay of the land, she began each project with clear direction from her manager and worked judiciously to complete her tasks.

Once Stacy finished her assignments and had no additional requests from her manager, she notified her colleagues that she was leaving and could be reached at home. Many days she would leave the office around 3:00 p.m. When her work was slow, she would arrive around 9:00 a.m.

After a few weeks, her colleagues began to complain to the manager about Stacy's lack of responsibility and her slacking by taking time off during work hours. They could not understand why the manager continued to allow such behavior. Was she the "golden child?" How could she possibly expect to keep her job when she did not put in at least eight hours in the office? To their surprise, the manager explained that Stacy had asked for a flexible work schedule and that she could easily work from home on some projects. He had found that as long as her productivity was above average, he had no problem with her request.

> **Question:** *Communication differences were abundant in this story; list at least two and how you would have handled things differently.*
>
> **Question:** *Name the person or persons in this story that valued work/life balance.*
>
> **Question:** *What mistake did Stacy make, if any? How about her manager?*
>
> *Hint from Doc B—Don't forget that a large part of the workforce believes that you must physically be present to be at work.*

Once upon a time in a land not so far away . . .
Fran was the head of nursing for a large regional hospital. She had been a practicing nurse for many years and had moved into management some twenty years ago. It seemed like every year it got tougher and tougher to keep the young nurse recruits much beyond their completed training, and with the cost of training only increasing, this loss of investment dollars simply could not continue.

Most of her supervisory nurses had been with the hospital for a very long time and had lots of seniority. They had run their floors efficiently and provided good care for their patients. Fran knew that in today's competitive market, they needed to do better. Her goal was to improve two critical elements: patient care and nursing staff retention. Fran called a special Nurse Supervisory meeting to solicit ideas and input from her supervisory nurses. Most of the supervisors were very defensive regarding the quality of their patient care (to be expected) because after all, they had been doing this for many years! With regards to the nurse retention, Fran could not take their complaints fast enough.

Comments such as, "They expect to only administer medication, forward requests to the orderlies, take breaks, and chat up the doctors—not empty bed pans!" They explained that they had their rules and procedures, and they were to be followed to the letter. The young nurses' suggestions were silly and not to be taken seriously. Many of the supervisors felt that the young nurses just did not want to work very hard and that they (the supervisors) were doing most of the work. Fran was certain that this kind of attitude would clearly block the change that was needed. She wanted solutions, not excuses!

Question: *What is the first thing that you would do if you were Fran? (Besides firing all of her nurse supervisors.)*

Question: *Why were the new nurses quitting just after they completed their training?*

Question: *What could the older nurses do to provide solutions instead of complaints?*

***Hint from Doc B**—Change is hard for most of us, but flexibility is the number one "must haves" on all of my clients' lists.*

Once upon a time in a place not so far away . . .
There lived a very young CEO who led a prosperous and progressive advertising and public relation firm which employed over 150 people. She was known to be the most successful young entrepreneur in the city and was fortunate to be able to recruit the best and the brightest from major universities all over the state. The average age at her firm was early thirties, and many young staffers were in their early twenties. Creativity was their primary ingredient for success, and ideas flowed easily throughout the organization.

Virtual meetings were the norm; technology was the critical element of any and all client presentations. The company motto was "work hard and play hard," which accounted for the pool table and video games in the company break room, the refrigerator stocked with power drinks, and continual video streaming on numerous monitors throughout the facility. Employees were encouraged to work at all hours of the day or night, whatever suited their needs.

One day, the CEO received a call from one of their major clients. This client had recently hired a very seasoned executive to lead their Marketing and Advertising division, and he was requesting a meeting. Our CEO said that she could set up for a virtual meeting as soon as the client was ready, but to her surprise, the new Marketing and Advertising executive said he preferred face-to-face meetings. Could they be ready with a full presentation of their services and deliverables by the end of the week? The CEO said no problem and the meeting was set. She notified her team of the upcoming meeting and what needed to be prepared. She was certain that they would "wow" this new executive, as they were the best in the business.

The CEO and three of her best associates arrived at the client's office just a little after the scheduled 9:00 a.m. meeting. They were escorted into the conference room and began setting up for the presentation. Immediately, the new Marketing and Advertising executive entered and introduced himself and sat silently while the team finished getting ready for the presentation. The CEO offered no apologies for being late. She also neglected to remind her three associates to dress appropriately for this meeting, and they looked young and inexperienced in their T-shirts and casual clothing.

Although the presentation was impressive, the Marketing and Advertising executive was concerned about the lack of business maturity with this team. He was not sure that this was the right firm to handle his company's business. He needed a firm that respected his time and understood his needs. Perhaps it was time to make a change.

> **Question:** *What is the risk of not having a more diverse workforce?*
>
> **Question:** *What kind of needs would you think the executive was referring to?*
>
> **Question:** *Name three major mistakes made by the CEO and how would you have corrected them.*
>
> ***Hint from Doc B**—Sometimes we tend to think everyone lives in our world; each generation must understand other worlds are out there.*

Not all stories have happy endings. In most of these cases, once the issues were clearly identified (usually by a third party like me) and each generation began to realize their specific contribution to the problem, understood their unique strengths and differences, and figured out that different was a good thing, workable solutions were created. The involved parties had to remember that the goal is to be heard, not to always speak, that everyone wants to be respected and have their work acknowledged, and most importantly, everyone needs to feel valued by their managers and colleagues. When these areas are addressed, it becomes much easier to see that we are much more alike than we are different.

Your Prescription Is ...

Enjoy and embrace how fantastically unique each and every one of us are. Laugh at yourself every once in a while and identify at least one positive thing you like about each person you work with. When times get tense, take out your list and review!

—Doctor B

Notes

Notes

CHAPTER EIGHT

Making "Shift" Happen!

Getting things done at work, efficiently and if possible, pleasurably, is the name of the game. That's right, pleasurably! After all, most companies are in the business of making a profit (if not-for-profit, making sure a service, product, or cause is delivered effectively). There is no rule in business about not enjoying the work that you do.

We spend the majority of our time on this earth working, mostly because we need money to live our lives, and for many the work itself becomes our lives. Whatever your particular situation, life is too short to not have some fun at work! Knowing that you contributed to something bigger than yourself and that you are acknowledged for that contribution can go a long way to feeling worthwhile in your job.

You have probably heard the term *people skills* over and over again from the time you interviewed for your first job to your last annual performance review. I am often asked, "What exactly are people skills?" Some think people skills simply mean that they must like people. Others feel that having a lot of friends indicates that they have obtained this skill set.

In my experience, people skills represent the ability to understand and communicate effectively with all kinds of people. That includes those that do not look or sound like you and those that may not believe what you do or react the way you do; those that don't value the same things you do or expect the same things you do; or coworkers that may not have the same work habits that you do or make decisions the same way you do.

The absolute best you can do is to first acknowledge the differences and then try to understand them. Try not to judge; instead, listen more effectively and to learn as much as you can about individuals. The good news is that each generation has given us a lot more than grief. Millennials have begun to bring true diversity to the workplace, embracing cultural and racial diversity as well as gender equality. Gen-Xers demanded work/life balance, and they demonstrated that technology makes it possible to work from anywhere. Boomers actually developed the technology that we are so dependent on today, and they are skilled at developing relationships. Veterans made it possible for the workplace to sustain the changes, and they have provided the wisdom that we all need to continue to lead the change.

More good news is that if you are going to spend the better part of your day together, each generation can eventually like one another; yes, *like one another*. I'm not referring to the lovefest at Woodstock or anything like that. I am simply saying that we can appreciate our individual differences and maybe even be motivated to change a few things that aren't working. Here is some food for thought:

> A twenty-three-year-old New York City currency trader said, "I dress more conservatively now; people take me more seriously when I do."

> A fifty-five-year-old Houston marketing director said, "I can't believe I am saying this, but I can actually understand how sending an email or having a conference call can be just as effective as having a team meeting."

> Just recently a thirty-two-year-old Dallas production manager told me,

"With all these young punks constantly surfing the net and texting their friends, I was certain they weren't getting any work done, but I was pleasantly surprised at the quality and creativity that they produced on a project, which they completed on time!"

My sixty-eight-year-old uncle recently commented, "I think the younger people coming into the workplace have the right idea; nobody wants to say that they wished they had worked more on their tombstone." He wished he could have a do-over for much of his work life.

Summary

As you can see, we can all learn a thing or two, and stereotypes are not always so true. Just remember, each new generation that enters the workplace faces the rituals and rules of the existing generational mix; and more than likely, the blending begins. As we have seen in history, some of the good and some of the bad remains, but all in all, each generation will mold the workplace of the future.

Your Prescription Is . . .

You know the saying referred to as KISS: "Keep it simple, stupid!" That is my motto whenever possible. I believe in learning and understanding the basics, and when the situation calls for a deeper sense of knowledge, go deep at that time. In keeping with this theory, I would like to share a simple cheat sheet—the Generational KISS Chart. I know everyone appreciates a good summary, and the following chart provides exactly that! And please remember, all of us want to be acknowledged for our value and respected at work no matter what generation we belong to; in this way we are really generation us! As a proud Boomer, my last words for you are: use it or lose it!

—Doctor B

The Generational KISS Chart

	VETERAN (65+)	BOOMER (46-64)	GEN-XER (30-45)	MILLENNIAL (18-29)
Work Ethic & Values	Hard work; respects authority; sacrifice; rules	Workaholics; personal fulfillment; question authority	Self-reliance; skeptical; wants structure & direction	What's next; multitasking; tenacity; tolerant
Work is...	An obligation	An exciting adventure	A contract	A means to an end
Leadership Style	Directive; command & control	Consensual; collegial	Everyone is the same; challenge others	To be determined
Interactive Style	Individual	Team; loves meetings	Entrepreneur	Participative
Communications	Formal; memo form	Face-to-face	Direct and immediate	E-mail; texting
Feedback & Rewards	No news is good news; satisfaction is a job well done	Don't appreciate feedback; money and title recognition	How am I doing? Freedom is the best reward	Whenever I want it; meaningful work
Motivating Messages	Your experience is respected	You are valued & needed	Do it your way and forget the rules	You will work with other bright & creative people
Work & Family Life	Ne're the twin shall meet	No balance; work to live	Balance	Balance

Information provided by "Mixing and Managing Four Generations of Employees" by Greg Hammill

Notes

Notes

References

Hammill, Greg. "Mixing and Managing Four Generations of Employees" *FDU Magazine*, Winter/Spring 2005.

Karp, Hank; Fuller, Connie; Sirias, Danilo. *Bridging the Boomer Xer Gap: Creating Authentic Teams for High Performance at Work*, Palo Alto, Calif.: Davies-Black Publishing, 2002.

Kersten, Denise. ""Today's Generations Face New Communication Gap," *USA Today*, November 15, 2002.

Lancaster, Lynne C.; Stillman, David. *When Generations Collide: Who They Are, Why They Clash, How to Solve the Generational Puzzle at Work*. Harper Collins Publishers Inc., 2002.

Sago, Brad. "Uncommon Threads: Mending the Generation Gap at Work," Executive Update, July 2000.

Walston, Sandra Ford. *Distinguishing Communication Approaches Across Generations* (online publication).

Zemke, Ron; Raines, Claire; Filipczak, Bob. *Generations at Work: Managing the Clash of Veterans, Boomers, Xers and Nexters in Your*

Workplace. New York, N.Y.; American Management Association, 2000.

Raines, Claire. *Connecting Generations: The Sourcebook*

Murphy, Mark. "Managing Generation "Why?" (online article from leadership IQ).

Mithers, Carol. "Workplace Wars" article in *Ladies Home Journal*, May 2009.

ABOUT THE AUTHOR

BONNIE DELESANDRI MONYCH is the president and a founder of The New WorkPlace Inc., a human capital strategy firm that helps clients link people to profits and possibilities. Also known as Your WorkPlace Doctor (Doctor B), she is a passionate people strategist and business analyst who provides straightforward and bottom line consulting support in the areas Strategic Talent Planning, Human Capital Forensics and Risk Analysis, Leadership Assessment & Development, Team Development and Group Performance, Diversity & Inclusion, and Employee Crisis Management. She is also considered to be a "cutting-edge expert" on the subject of Generations in the Workplace. She has coached thousands of individuals on how to achieve an effective and rewarding career path.

Doctor B has been featured on the local CBS network and Clear Channel Sunny 99FM radio sharing her "Career Tip of the Week" for several years. She has delivered keynote addresses on various topics including Working with Four Generations; Networking Girl Style—How to Extend Your Reach Without a Golf Club; Me, Inc—How to be the CEO of your Career; and Who Are You? She published her first book, *Shift Happens: Straight Talk About Jobs, Work and*

Careers in 1996, which was updated and reprinted in 2000. She is currently working on her third book, *God Works, Inc.: HE Wants You to be the CEO of Your Career.*

She is a native Texan, raised two daughters and now enjoys the freedom of spoiling her two beautiful granddaughters. Doctor B is very active in her community, volunteering at the Woodlands Church job support ministry. She is a member of the Texas Diversity Council and has chaired the Women in Leadership Symposium as well as the Diversity Awards Luncheon. Doctor B also supports the growth of the business community by being an active member of the Greater Houston Partnership's Advocate Committee and CEO Roundtable.

Contact her at:
www.yourworkplacedoctor.com

You might also enjoy Doctor B's first book:

"Shift"Happens,
Straight Talk about Jobs, Work, and Careers